Learning to Read, Step by Step!

Ready to Read   Preschool–Kindergarten
• big type and easy words • rhyme and rhythm • picture clues
For children who know the alphabet and are eager to begin reading.

Reading with Help   Preschool–Grade 1
• basic vocabulary • short sentences • simple stories
For children who recognize familiar words and sound out new words with help.

Reading on Your Own   Grades 1–3
• engaging characters • easy-to-follow plots • popular topics
For children who are ready to read on their own.

Reading Paragraphs   Grades 2–3
• challenging vocabulary • short paragraphs • exciting stories
For newly independent readers who read simple sentences with confidence.

Ready for Chapters   Grades 2–4
• chapters • longer paragraphs • full-color art
For children who want to take the plunge into chapter books but still like colorful pictures.

STEP INTO READING® is designed to give every child a successful reading experience. The grade levels are only guides; children will progress through the steps at their own speed, developing confidence in their reading. The F&P Text Level on the back cover serves as another tool to help you choose the right book for your child.

Remember, a lifetime love of reading starts with a single step!

For Sandra and Robert
—N.H.
For Theo and his chums
—J.K.

Text copyright © 2004 by Nina Hess. Illustrations copyright © 2004 by John Kanzler.
All rights reserved. Published in the United States by Random House Children's Books, a
division of Random House LLC, a Penguin Random House Company, New York.

Step into Reading, Random House, and the Random House colophon are registered trademarks of
Random House LLC.

Visit us on the Web!
StepIntoReading.com
randomhouse.com/kids

Educators and librarians, for a variety of teaching tools, visit us at
RHTeachersLibrarians.com

Library of Congress Cataloging-in-Publication Data
Hess, Nina.
Whose feet? / by Nina Hess ; illustrated by John Kanzler. — 1st ed.
   p.   cm. — (Step into reading. A step 2 book)
Summary: Introduces feet and describes how their differences allow animals to do special
things, such as a mole's long, thick claws that are made for digging and a bat's strong feet that
can hook into rocks.
ISBN 978-0-375-82623-8 (trade) — ISBN 978-0-375-92623-5 (lib. bdg.)
1. Foot—Juvenile literature. 2. Animals—Juvenile literature. [1. Foot. 2. Animals.]
I. Kanzler, John, ill. II. Title. III. Series.
QL950.7 .H47 2004 591.47'9—dc22 2003011682

Printed in the United States of America
10 9 8

This book has been officially leveled by using the F&P Text Level Gradient™ Leveling System.

Whose Feet?

by Nina Hess

illustrated by John Kanzler

Random House New York

Feet can dig.
Long, thick claws
poke out of these toes.
These feet dig out
a brand-new home.

Whose feet can dig?

Mole feet!
Mole feet are made
for digging.
Their claws work
like shovels.

They help moles
build a cozy place
to sleep underground.

Feet can dash.
On the hunt,
these feet go fast.

They leap. They dash.
They will not slide.
Whose feet can dash?

Cheetah feet!
Cheetah feet are
like soccer cleats.

They have thick pads
and short, strong claws.

This keeps cheetahs
from slipping as they
race to catch their prey.

Feet can hop.

Danger comes.

No time to wait.

These feet hop
to find a hiding place.
Whose feet can hop?

Bunny feet!

When scared,
bunnies do not run.
Instead, they hop.

Their long feet
make strong springs.
Strong springs mean
a fast getaway!

Feet can hang.
Right side up,
these feet look frail.

But upside down,
these feet hang on tight.
Whose feet can hang?

Bat feet!

They are like tiny hooks.

Most bats cannot stand.

Their legs are too weak.

But bat feet are strong.
They can hang
from branches, beams,
and even holes in rocks!

Feet can splash.
Time to grab a snack
down deep.

These feet splash
and flip upside down.
Whose feet can splash?

Duck feet!
Duck feet have skin
between their toes.

These webbed feet
act like paddles.
They help ducks
flip and swim
under the water.
There, ducks can snatch
bits of grass to eat.

Feet can swing.

Back and forth,
side to side,
these feet swing
from vine to vine.
Whose feet can swing?

Orangutan feet!

Orangutan feet have
five long toes.
One of them
faces sideways.

It is almost
like a thumb!
This special toe
lets them grab hold
and swing away!

Whose feet can dig?

Whose feet can dash?

Whose feet can hop?

Whose feet can hang?

Whose feet can splash?

Whose feet can swing?

Whose feet?

Your feet!

Your feet have
ten toes and
fifty-two bones.

They are made
for walking,
jumping, and running.
But that is not all!

How many
different things
can YOUR feet do?

STEP 2 · READING WITH HELP

Have you read these Step into Reading books?

Put a check next to each one you've read!

STEP 3 · READING ON YOUR OWN

Are you ready for the next Step?

For activities, information about Common Core, and more books to read, visit
StepIntoReading.com

2
STEP — READING WITH HELP

STEP INTO READING®

Whose feet scrape? Whose feet splash?
Find out in this book all about feet!

Learning to Read, Step by Step!

1 Ready to Read   **Preschool–Kindergarten**

2 Reading with Help   **Preschool–Grade 1**
Does your child recognize familiar words on sight and
sound out new words with help? Step 2 is just right.
Basic Vocabulary • Short Sentences • Simple Stories

3 Reading on Your Own   **Grades 1–3**

4 Reading Paragraphs   **Grades 2–3**

5 Ready for C

F&P TEXT LEVEL I

US $3.99 / $4.99 CAN

ISBN 978-0-375-82623-8

50399

RANDOM HOUSE
StepIntoReading.com

the ESSENTIAL OIL TRUTH

THE FACTS WITHOUT THE HYPE

SECOND EDITION

PQJ846846

JEN O'SULLIVAN